Laugh 'n' Ride

A SpongeBob Joke Book

NICKELODEON®

SpongeBob SquarePants®

Laugh 'n' Ride

A SpongeBob Joke Book

by David Lewman

SCHOLASTIC INC.

New York Toronto London Auckland Sydney
Mexico City New Delhi Hong Kong Buenos Aires

SpongeBob ran up to Patrick's rock. "Patrick!" he called. "It's time for the Annual Jellyfishing Convention! We're going on a trip!"

"Oh, boy! A trip!" cried Patrick. "Let's go RIGHT NOW!"

SpongeBob smiled. "Hold on, Patrick. First we have to pack."

"Uh . . . what do we have to pack?" asked Patrick.

"Well, let's see . . . underwear, toothbrush, pajamas—," SpongeBob started to say.

"That doesn't sound like fun, SpongeBob," Patrick said.

"Yeah, but we can tell each other jokes while we pack!" SpongeBob said. "Like this one: What did the little sponge keep asking his parents on their trip?"

"I dunno . . . ," said Patrick.

"Are we square yet?" answered SpongeBob, and the two friends cracked up. "Now it's your turn."

"Uh . . . what kind of pants can you make out of a suitcase?" asked Patrick. Before SpongeBob could answer, Patrick excitedly shouted out, "Baggy pants! Get it?"

So SpongeBob and Patrick packed their backpacks and told jokes.

Why did the duck miss his bus?

He was up all night quacking.

QUACK!
QUACK!
QUACK!

What does Gary pack before a trip?

His sluggage.

Where does Mr. Krabs keep his bags?

Under his eyes.

Why was the clown up late the night before his trip?

He was packing his gags.

What do traveling dogs carry their clothes in?

Barkpacks.

What do you say when you can't decide whether to travel or pig out?

"Trip or treat!"

8

Why didn't Mrs. Puff visit the puzzle museum?

She didn't want to go to pieces.

What do cows like to visit on their vacations?

The *mooseums*.

Which part of a trip do combs like best?

Departing.

Why did the ice cream keep diving into the root beer?

He loved to fizz it!

Why did the tourist visit haunted houses?

He loved frightseeing.

THREE
HOURS
LATER

Once they had packed their backpacks, SpongeBob and Patrick went to the Bikini Bottom bus station to buy tickets. But when they got to the station, there was a long line of fish waiting at the ticket window.

"Oh no, SpongeBob, we're going to have to wait in line forever!" Patrick whined.

"Don't worry, Patrick," SpongeBob asked. "We could do something fun."

Patrick grinned. "Like build a house of cards?"

"Or tell each other more jokes!" SpongeBob said.
"Knock, knock."

"Who's there?" answered Patrick.

"Sleeve."

"Sleeve who?"

"Let's leave and go on a trip!" SpongeBob shouted,
and the pair laughed and laughed till they both teared
up. Even some of the folks in line giggled.

SpongeBob and Patrick started to trade more jokes.

Why did the traveler wad his boarding pass up into a ball?

He wanted a round-trip ticket.

Why don't bowlers mind flat tires?

They can always get a spare.

What do ghosts buy when they travel?
Boo-venirs.

What do mosquitoes write when they go on vacation?

Pestcards.

Why did the tourist punch the street?

He wanted to hit the road.

What do you call a pig running down a highway?

A road hog.

Why did Mrs. Puff's class keep letting all the other classes go first?

They were on a yield trip.

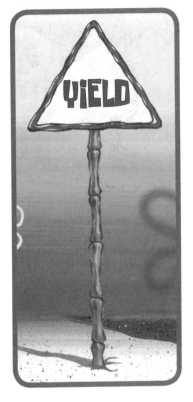

How did the road feel when a potato snack landed on it?

Like it had a chip on its shoulder.

What's the difference between a concrete path and a big stocking?

One's a sidewalk and the other's a wide sock.

What's the difference between a tour book and a wave full of pebbles?

One's a travel guide and the other's a gravel tide.

TEN HOURS LATER

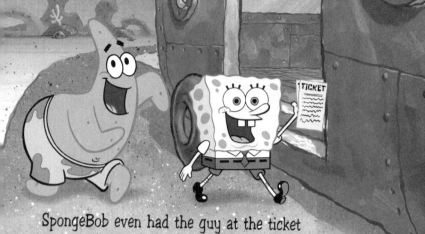

SpongeBob even had the guy at the ticket window laughing when he told this joke. "Why did the traveler wear his swimsuit for the road trip?" asked SpongeBob.

The ticket-window guy shrugged.

"He'd heard they were going in a carpool!" SpongeBob said, and everyone clapped.

"That was funny," the ticket-window guy said. "And just for making me laugh, you get two tickets for the price of one."

Patrick and SpongeBob couldn't believe it. "Thanks!" they said.

They climbed up the steps of the bus that would take them to the convention, and found seats in the back. After about two minutes Patrick asked, "Are we square yet? I mean, are we there yet? Ha-ha-ha-ha!"

"Nope," said SpongeBob. "It's going to be a while before we get to the convention."

"Auggghhh!" Patrick groaned. "Long drives are BORING!"

"Not if we tell each other certain somethings," SpongeBob said, giggling.

"Like what?" Patrick asked.

"Jokes!" answered SpongeBob.

How did the pair of penguins travel?

On an icicle built for two.

Why did Sandy slide down the mountain on her vacation?

She wanted to go sight-skiing.

21

When is a wave like a car coming to a stop?

When it breaks.

Why did the actor refuse to slow down until the end of her trip?

She was waiting for her big brake.

22

Why did Mr. Krabs cover his lawn with a white canvas?

He wanted to have a yard sail.

Which oar is no good for rowing a boat?

A dinosaur.

23

What do you call it when two oars fall in love?

True row-mance.

How do sailors choose who has to man the oars?

"Eeny, meeny, miny, row."

What happened to the spuds who went canoeing?

They became splashed potatoes.

Why do cars lie?

They can always get someone to back them up.

What does Mr. Krabs like to drive?

A hard bargain.

What kind of driving is SpongeBob best at?

Driving Squidward crazy.

What happened to the basketball player who took a vacation?

He was called for traveling.

Why do basketball players need cars?

So they can drive to the basket.

TEN MINUTES LATER

SpongeBob and Patrick were riding happily along when suddenly they heard a loud *klunk!* The bus rolled to a stop, and the driver got out to look under the hood. Smoke rose from the engine.

"Engine's busted," drawled the driver. "Looks like we're stuck."

"But the Jellyfishing Convention is about to start!" cried SpongeBob.

The driver pushed his hat back and scratched his forehead. "Well, it's not that much farther," he said. "You could walk."

Moments later SpongeBob and Patrick were trudging down the road with their backpacks. "I have an idea, Patrick. We could tell more jokes," SpongeBob suggested.

"Exactly what I was thinking," Patrick agreed, "except my idea had sandwiches in it."

Which part of a camera travels the fastest?

The zoom lens.

When is gasoline like the fish at Mussel Beach?

When it's pumped.

Which reptile is the best at reading maps?

The navi*gator*.

What sign does Mr. Krabs always stop for?

The dollar sign.

When is a baseball team like a traveler looking for a bathroom?

When it needs a shortstop.

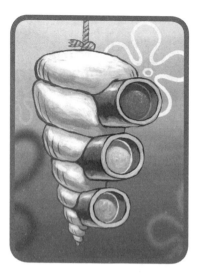

How is a cork like a traffic light?

They're both stoppers.

Why does SpongeBob refuse to turn left?

He always wants to do the right thing.

Why did the banana stick its hand out?

It was about to make a ripe turn.

Why does seawater always get to touch the shore first?

It has the right-of-wave.

Where do bees start their trips?

At the buzz station.

33

Which restaurant worker knows the most about transportation?

The busboy.

What do you call a tortoise with a camera?

A snapping turtle.

Why did the mummy pull off the road?

To go to the rest tomb.

TWO
DAYS
LATER

When SpongeBob and Patrick finally reached the Jellyfishing Convention, there was a long line to get in.

"Not another line!" Patrick wailed. "I'm tired of waiting

"Are you tired of jokes?" SpongeBob asked.

Patrick grinned. "Never! And I've got one for you. Knock, knock."

"Who's there?" answered SpongeBob.

"Turnip."

"Turnip who?"

"Turn up here, I need a rest stop," Patrick replied, as t two of them fell down laughing.

Why was Patrick chasing his clock?

It was running fast.

What kind of boat never sets sail?

A gravy boat.

S.S. CHEAPSKATE

Why was the sailor sad at the end of his voyage?

He missed the boat.

What do sailors eat for breakfast?

Boatmeal.

Why did the spud jump in the ocean?

He wanted to be a potato ship.

Why do old cars go on so many dates?

They're always getting fixed up.

What's a Krabby Patty's favorite way to travel?

Taking the fry way.

THE NEXT DAY

The next day SpongeBob and Patrick left the Jellyfishing Convention loaded down with souvenirs. "That was the greatest Annual Jellyfishing Convention ever!" SpongeBob exclaimed.

"Yeah!" Patrick agreed. "And the best part is now we don't have to take a long, boring bus ride back home!"

SpongeBob shook his head. "No, Patrick. We *do* have to take a long, boring bus ride back home! But it doesn't have to be boring!"

Patrick brightened up. "Jokes?" he asked hopefully.

"Of course!" SpongeBob answered, grinning.

Which part of the car is Patrick's favorite?

The grub compartment.

Why did Plankton do a somersault on the windshield?

He wanted to roll down the window.

Why was Patrick afraid of taking the highway?

He heard you had to pay the troll.

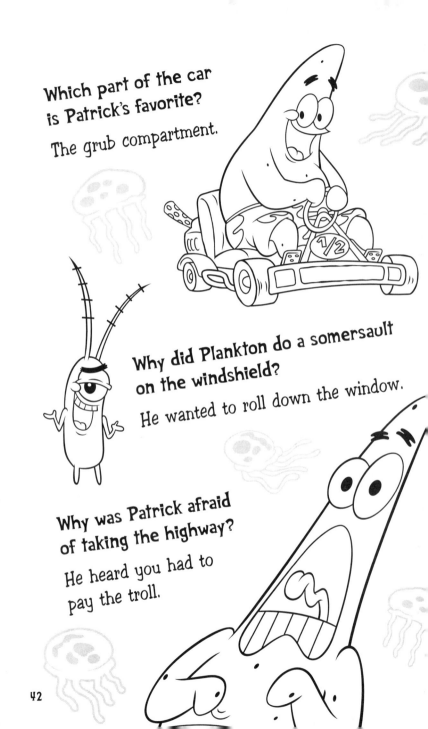

Where do chickens
buy gas?

At a cluck stop.

Why did the mongoose pull off the highway?

He wanted to stop for a little snake.

What do you spread on a hot, toasty road?

Traffic jam.

Why did the top get in the car?

He wanted to go for a spin.

What has strings, a handle, and a powerful engine?

A tennis rocket.

What has four legs, white wool, and a powerful engine?

A rocket sheep.

What's the difference between Sandy in space and SpongeBob in water?

One goes into orbit and the other can absorb it.

What do teeth ride down the highway?

Molarcycles.

What do skunks ride down the highway?

Odorcycles.

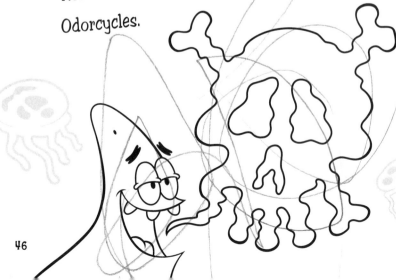

SIX
HOURS
LATER

At the end of the long bus ride SpongeBob and Patrick were finally back in Bikini Bottom. "Great trip, eh, buddy?" SpongeBob asked as they walked home.

"It sure was!" Patrick agreed.

"What was your favorite part?"

"The jokes!" Patrick shouted.

"You're right, Patrick," SpongeBob said. "And I've got one more for you: What did the pig say at the end of his trip?"

Patrick stared blankly. "There's no place like ham."